WORLD'S GREATEST
CLASSIC COUNTRY SONGS

73 of the Most Popular Country Classics Ever Written

From the Grand Ole Opry to the Wild West, this collection contains all your favorite classic country songs. Included are hits made famous by icons of the '40s and '50s like Hank Williams and Patsy Cline, as well as modern-day favorites from Garth Brooks and Alan Jackson. "High Noon" by legendary western star Tex Ritter, Debby Boone's inspirational "You Light Up My Life," and Marty Robbins's saga "El Paso" are just a few of the dozens of classics you'll find in this memorable collection.

Alfred Publishing Co., Inc.
16320 Roscoe Blvd., Suite 100
P.O. Box 10003
Van Nuys, CA 91410-0003
alfred.com

Cover Photos
Wagon Wheel Guitar: © istockphoto / Scott Leigh • Cowboy: © istockphoto / Doug Sims
• Upright Piano: © istockphoto / Donald Blais • Colorado Barn: © istockphoto / Ben Klaus

CONTENTS

ANY TIME

Words and Music by
HERBERT HAPPY LAWSON

Moderately

ANY DAY NOW

Words and Music by
BURT BACHARACH and BOB HILLIARD

BACK IN THE SADDLE AGAIN

Words and Music by
GENE AUTRY and RAY WHITLEY

10

BEHIND CLOSED DOORS

Words and Music by
KENNY O'DELL

all o - ver me in a crowd,_____ 'cause

peo - ple like to talk,_____ Lord, don't they love___ to talk.

But when they turn out the___ lights, I know she'll be leav - in'_____ with

me.

Chorus:

And when we get be - hind closed____

Verse 2:
My baby makes me smile, Lord, don't she make me smile.
She's never far away or too tired to say I want you.
She's always a lady, just like a lady should be.
But when they turn out the lights, she's still a baby to me.
(To Chorus:)

BOUQUET OF ROSES

Words and Music by
STEVE NELSON and BOB HILLIARD

Bouquet of Roses - 3 - 1

A BOY NAMED SUE

Words and Music by
SHEL SILVERSTEIN

Verse I

(Recitation) Well, my daddy left home when I was three, and he didn't leave much to ma and me, Just this old guitar and an empty bottle of booze.

Now, I don't blame him because he run and hid, but the meanest thing that he

A Boy Named Sue - 3 - 1

Verse II

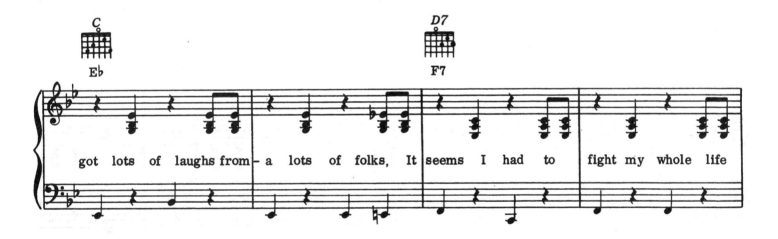

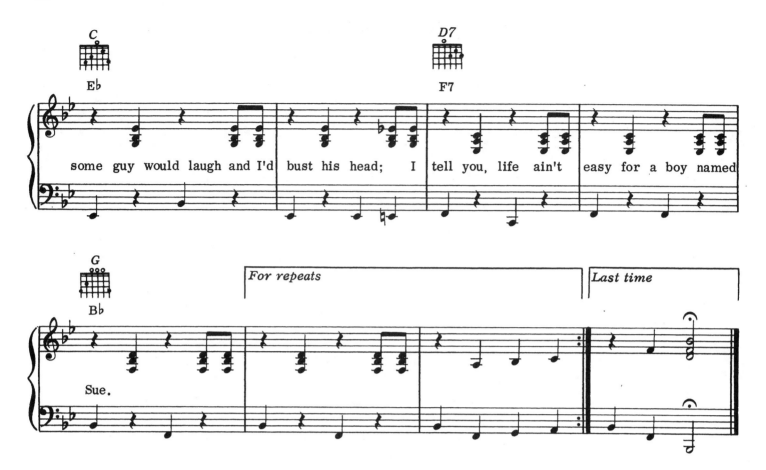

3. (Well,) I grew up quick and I grew up mean, My fist got hard and my wits got keen,
   Roamed from town to town to hide my shame. But I made me a vow to the moon and stars:
   I'd search the honky tonks and bars and kill that man that give me that awful name.

4. But it was Gatlinburg in mid-July and I had just hit town and my throat was dry,
   I'd thought I'd stop and have myself a brew. At an old saloon on a street of mud
   And at a table dealing stud sat the dirty, mangy dog that named me Sue.

5. Well, I knew that snake was my own sweet dad from a worn-out picture that my mother had,
   And I knew that scar on his cheek and his evil eye. He was big and bent and gray and old,
   And I looked at him and my blood ran cold, and I said "My name is Sue. How do you do.
   Now you're gonna die." Yeah, that's what I told him.

6. Well, I hit him right between the eyes and he went down, but to my surprise he come up with a knife
   And cut off a piece of my ear. But I busted a chair right across his teeth, And we crashed through
   the wall and into the street, Kicking and a-gouging in the mud and the blood and the beer.

7. I tell you I've fought tougher men but I really can't remember when,
   He kicked like a mule and he bit like a crocodile. I heard him laughin' and then I heard him cussin',
   He went for his gun and I pulled mine first. He stood there looking at me and I saw him smile.

8. And he said, "Son, this world is rough and if a man's gonna make it, he's gotta be tough;
   And I knew I wouldn't be there to help you along. So I give you that name and I said 'Goodbye;'
   I knew you'd have to get tough or die. And it's that name that helped to make you strong."

9. "Yeah," he said, "Now you have just fought one helluva fight, and I know you hate me and you've
   got the right to kill me now, and I wouldn't blame you if you do. But you ought to thank me
   before I die for the gravel in your guts and the spit in your eye because I'm the _ _ _ _
   that named you Sue."

   Yeah, what could I do? What could I do?

10. I got all choked up and I threw down my gun. Called him a pa and he called me a son,
    And I come away with a different point of view. And I think about him now and then.
    Every time I tried, every time I win and if I ever have a son I think I am gonna name him
    Bill or George — anything but Sue.

COOL WATER

Words and Music by
BOB NOLAN

22

Cool Water - 3 - 2

Verse 2:
The nights are cool and I'm a fool, each star's a pool of water, cool water.
But with the dawn I'll wake and yawn and carry on to water, cool, clear water.
(To Chorus:)

Verse 3:
The shadows sway and seem to say, "Tonight we pray for water, cool water."
And way up there He'll hear our pray'r and show us where there's water, cool, clear water.
(To Chorus:)

Verse 4:
Dan's feet are sore, he's yearning for just one thing more than water, cool water.
Like me, I guess he'd like to rest where there's no quest for water, cool, clear water.
(To Chorus:)

CRYING IN THE CHAPEL

Slowly, with expression

Words and Music by
ARTIE GLENN

Lyrics under the staves:

First system:
We___ gath - er in the chap - el,___ just to sing and praise the
Your___ bur - dens will be light - er,___ and you'll sure - ly find the

Chords (first system): A7 D7 Fm6 G7 D7 Dm7/G

Second system:
1.
Lord.   2. Ev - 'ry sin - ner looks for

Chords (second system): C Dm7 G7 N.C.

Third system:
2.
way.___

Chords (third system): C F C F7 C C6

THE DANCE

Words and Music by
TONY ARATA

The Dance - 3 - 1

DEVIL WOMAN

Words and Music by
MARTY ROBBINS

Moderate rhumba ♩ = 132

1. I told Mar-y a-bout____ us.____ I told her a-bout__ our great

sin. Mar-y cried__ and for-gave____ me, and

Mar-y took me back a-gain.____ Said if I want-ed my

Devil Woman - 3 - 1

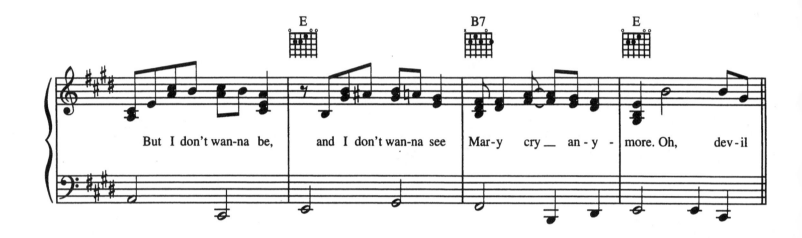

Chorus:

Devil Woman - 3 - 2

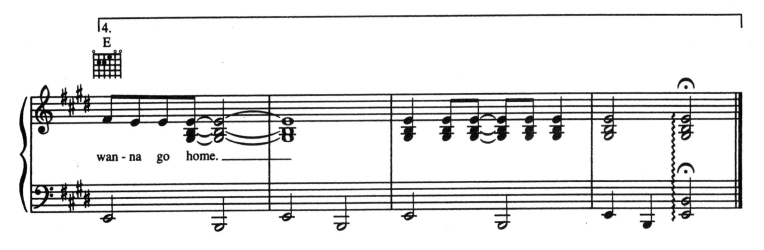

wan - na go home. _____

Verse 2:
Mary is waitin' and weepin'
Down in our shack by the sea.
Even after I've hurt her,
Mary's still in love with me.
Devil woman, it's over;
Trapped no more by your charms.
'Cause I don't wanna stay.
I wanna get away.
Woman, let go of my arm.
(To Chorus:)

Verse 3:
Devil woman, you're evil
Like the dark coral reef.
Like the winds that bring high tides,
You bring sorrow and grief.
You made me ashamed to face Mary.
Barely had the strength to tell.
Skies are not so black;
Mary took me back.
Mary has broken your spell.
(To Chorus:)

Verse 4:
Runnin' along by the seashore,
Runnin' as fast as I can.
Even the seagulls are happy,
Glad I'm comin' home again.
Never again will I ever
Cause another tear to fall.
Down the beach I see
What belongs to me,
The one I want most of all.
(To Chorus:)

DESPERADO

Words and Music by
DON HENLEY and GLENN FREY

Desperado - 6 - 1

o - pen the gate.___ It may be rain - in', but there's a

rain - bow a - bove you. ___ You bet - ter let some - bod - y love___ you,

you ___ bet - ter let some - bod - y love ___ you ___ be-

fore it's too ___ late.___

DON'T IT MAKE MY BROWN EYES BLUE

Words and Music by
RICHARD LEIGH

Don't It Make My Brown Eyes Blue - 3 - 1

DON'T FENCE ME IN

Words and Music by
COLE PORTER

* Alternate lyric.

Don't Fence Me In - 3 - 1

Refrain:

DON'T LET OUR LOVE START SLIPPIN' AWAY

Words and Music by
VINCE GILL and PETE WASNER

Moderately

Verse:

1. We've been up_____ all night long

2. *See additional lyrics*

tryin' to solve a prob-lem, hell, it's al - most dawn.

Don't Let Our Love Start Slippin' Away - 4 - 1

Ain't no time for sleep-in' if our love_ is wear-in' thin,

'cause I ain't giv-in' up___ and you ain't giv-in' in.

𝄋 *Chorus:*

Don't let our love start slip-pin', love start slip-pin' a - way.___

'Cause the life___ we've been liv - in' gets hard - er__ ev-er - y day.___

D.S. % al Coda

Repeat and fade

Verse 2:
A wounded love walks a real thin line,
And no communication will kill it every time.
So open up your heart, baby, we can work it out,
'Cause we've got the kind of love people dream about.
(To Chorus:)

DON'T UNDERESTIMATE MY LOVE FOR YOU

Words and Music by STEVE DIAMOND,
STEVE DORFF and DAVE LOGGINS

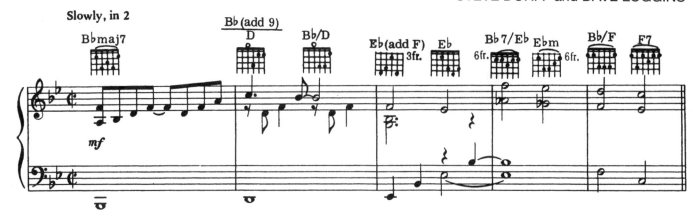

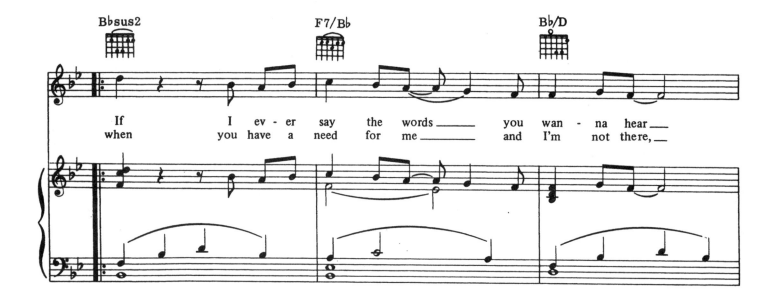

If I ev-er say the words _____ you wan-na hear _____
when you have a need for me _____ and I'm not there, _____

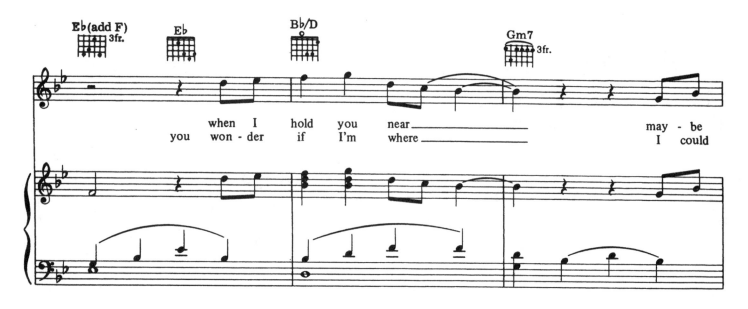

when I hold you near _____ may-be
you won-der if I'm where _____ I could

Don't Underestimate My Love For You - 6 - 1

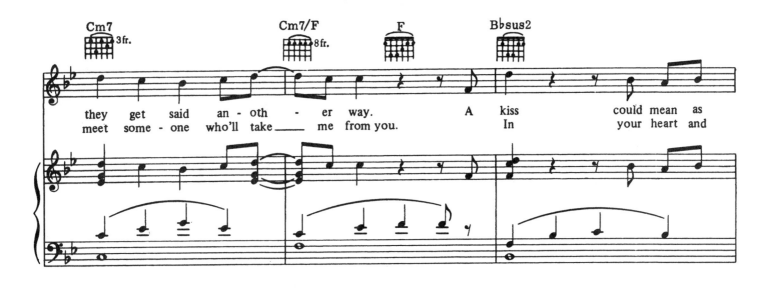

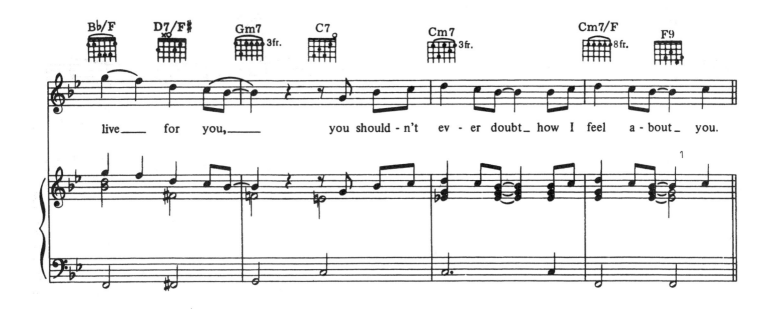

EIGHTEEN WHEELS AND A DOZEN ROSES

Words and Music by
GENE NELSON and PAUL NELSON

58

Repeat and fade

wheels _____ and a doz - en ros - es, ten more

Instrumental - to fade _____

miles _____ on his four - day run. A few more

songs _____ from the all night rad - i - o then he'll

spend the rest_ of his_ life with the one that he_ loves.

THE END OF THE WORLD

Words and Music by
ARTHUR KENT and SYLVIA DEE

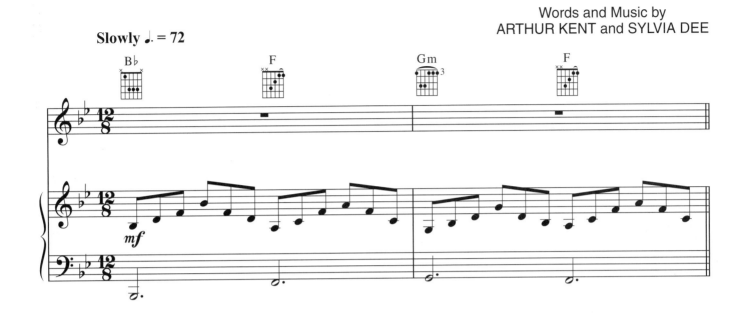

Verses 1 & 2:

1. Why_____ does the sun_____ go on shin - ing?_____
2. Why_____ do the birds_____ go on sing - ing?_____

Why_____ does the sea rush to shore?_____
Why_____ do the stars glow a - bove?_____

EL PASO

Words and Music by
MARTY ROBBINS

El Paso - 6 - 1

Bridge:

1. One night a wild young cow-boy came in, wild as the west Tex-as wind.
2. Out through the back door of Rose-'s I ran, out where the hors-es were tied.
3. I sad-dle up and a-way I did go, rid-ing a-lone in the dark.
4. Some-thing is dread-ful-ly wrong, for I feel a deep burn-ing pain in my side.

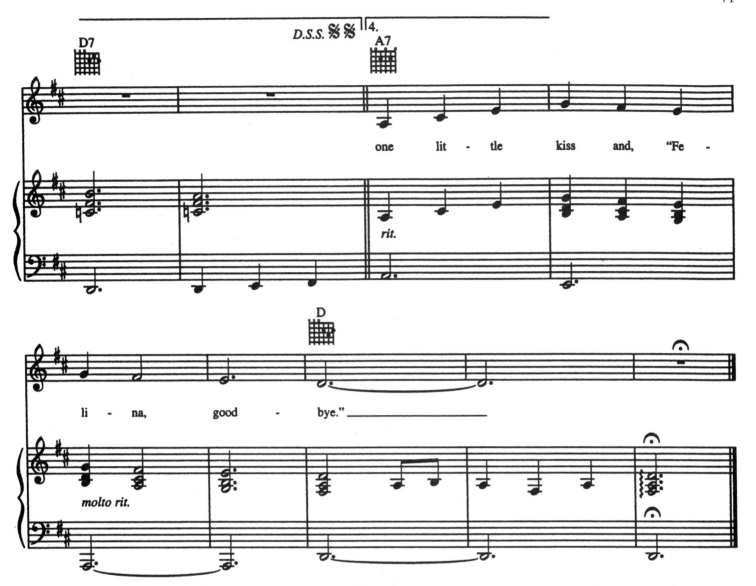

one lit - tle kiss and, "Fe -

li - na, good - bye." _____

Verse 5:
So, in anger, I challenged his right for the love of this maiden.
Down went his hand for the gun that he wore.

Verse 6:
My challenge was answered, in less than a heartbeat,
The handsome young stranger lay dead on the floor.

Verse 7:
Just for a moment I stood there in silence,
Shocked by the foul, evil deed I had done.

Verse 8:
Many thoughts raced through my mind as I stood there.
I had but one chance and that was to run.
(To Bridge 2:)

Verse 9:
. . . Just as fast as I could from the west Texas town of El Paso
Out to the badlands of New Mexico.

Verse 10:
Back in El Paso, my life would be worthless.
Everything's gone in life, nothing is left.

Verse 11:
It's been so long since I've seen the young maiden,
My love is stronger than my fear of death.
(To Bridge 3:)

FADED LOVE

Words and Music by
BOB WILLS and JOHNNIE LEE WILLS

Moderate country two-beat

Chorus:

I miss you, dar - lin', more and more__ ev - 'ry day,__

__ as heav - en would miss the stars__ a - bove.__

With ev - 'ry heart - beat I still think of you,__

__ and re - mem - ber our fad - ed love._____

Verse 2:
As I think of the past and all the pleasure we had,
As I watch the mating of the dove,
And it was in the springtime that we said goodbye.
I remember our faded love.
(To Chorus:)

A FEW OLE COUNTRY BOYS

Words and Music by
TROY SEALS and MENTOR WILLIAMS

Moderate country swing

Verse:

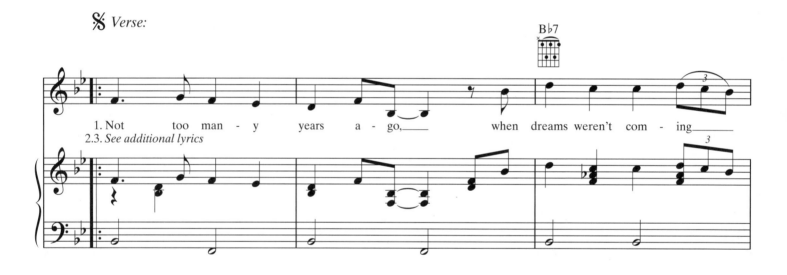

1. Not too man-y years a-go,____ when dreams weren't com-ing____
2.3. *See additional lyrics*

true, I'd reach for in-spi-ra-tion,__ some-times it would be

A Few Ole Country Boys - 4 - 1

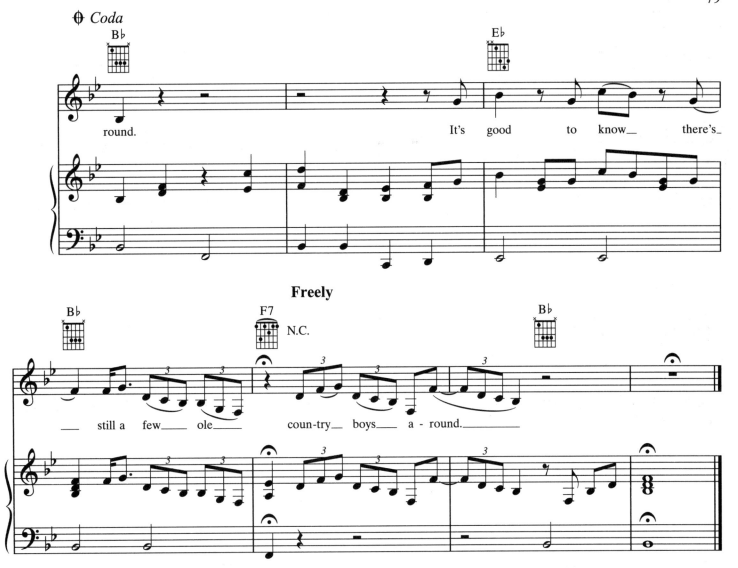

round. It's good to know__ there's_

still a few__ ole__ coun-try__ boys__ a - round._____

Freely

Verse 2:
From the smoke, it's hard to tell what's coming down the line.
We heard you were on the fast train comin' out of Caroline.
We wondered what you were haulin' when you rolled into town.
Say, it's good to know there's still a few ole country boys around.

Verse 3:
There's a lot of truth, you know, in our kind of songs,
About the life you're livin' and how love done you wrong.
As long as there's a jukebox and a honky-tonk in town.
It's good to know there's still a few ole country boys around.

FLOWERS ON THE WALL

Words and Music by
LEW DEWITT

Moderately

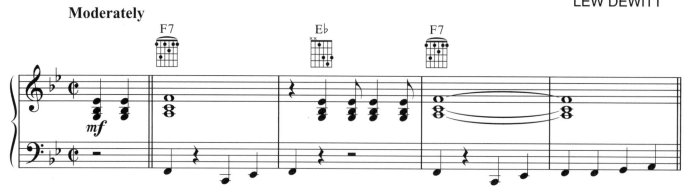

Verse:

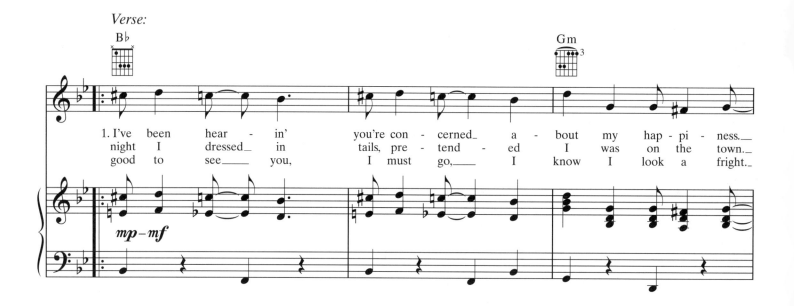

1. I've been hear-in' you're con - cerned a - bout my hap - pi - ness.
night I dressed in tails, pre - tend - ed I was on the town.
good to see you, I must go, I know I look a fright.

But all that thought you're giv - in' me is
As long as I can dream it's hard to
An - y way, my eyes are not ac -

FOUR WALLS

Words and Music by
MARVIN J. MOORE and GEORGE H. CAMPBELL, JR.

Slowly, with feeling

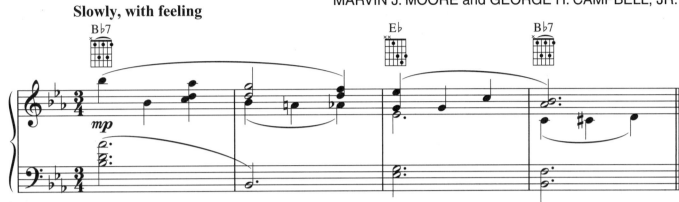

Verse:

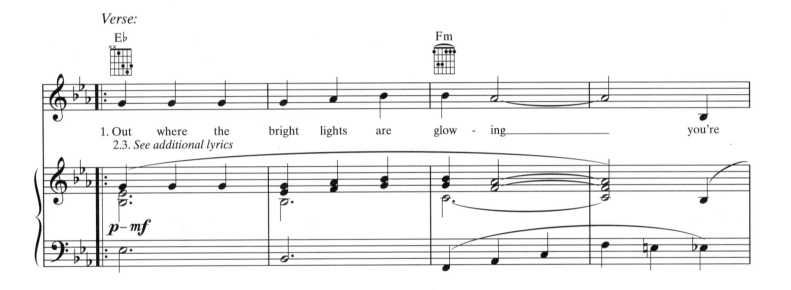

1. Out where the bright lights are glow - ing___ you're
2.3. *See additional lyrics*

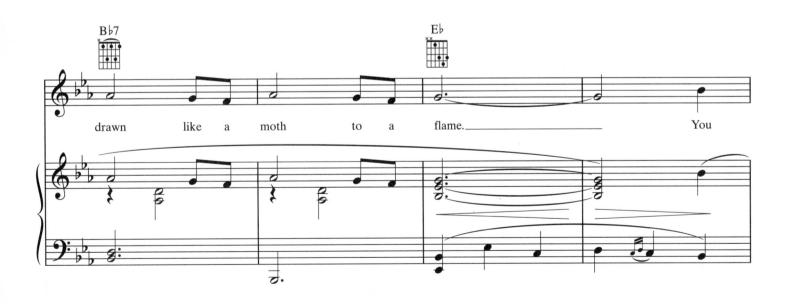

drawn like a moth to a flame.___ You

four walls too near me,
clos - ing in on me!
me!

Verse 2:
Sometimes I ask why I'm waiting,
But my walls have nothing to say.
I'm made for love, not for hating.
So here, where you left me, I'll stay.
(To Chorus:)

Verse 3:
One night with you is like heaven.
And so while I'm walking the floor,
I'll listen for steps in the hallway
And wait for your knock on my door.
(To Chorus:)

GO REST HIGH ON THAT MOUNTAIN

Words and Music by
VINCE GILL

Go Rest High on That Mountain - 3 - 1

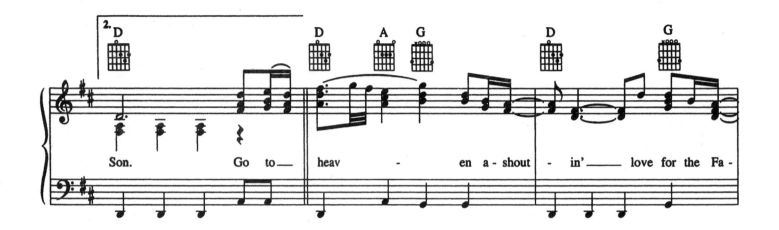

Son. Go to— heav - en a-shout - in'—— love for the Fa-

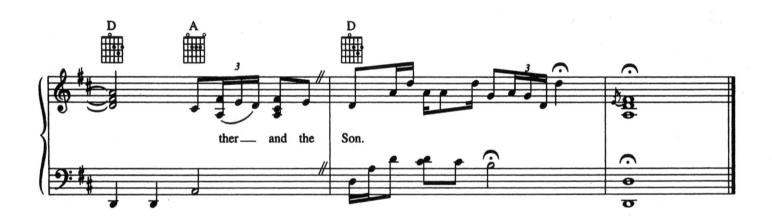

ther— and the Son.

Additional lyrics

2. Oh, how we cried the day you left us,
We gathered 'round your grave to grieve.
I wish I could see the angels' faces
When they hear your sweet voice sing.
(To Chorus)

I'M NOT READY YET

Words and Music by
TOM T. HALL

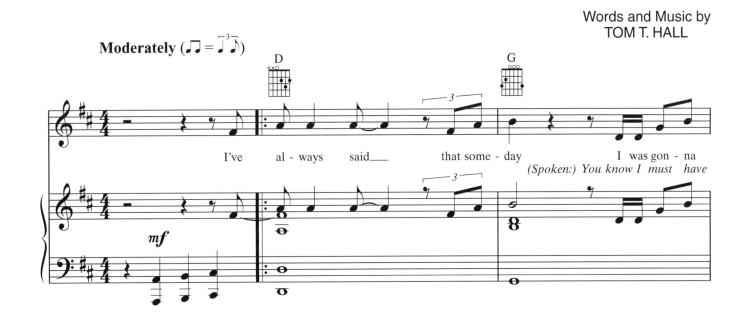

I've al-ways said___ that some-day I was gon - na
(Spoken:) You know I must have

leave you,
left you a hundred times, but you don't know that

some A - pril,
'cause I was afraid

when

all___ the land is wet,
I'd be ashamed that you'd laugh when you found out just how far I

some

GOOD OL' BOYS

Moderately Fast, with half-time feel

Words and Music by
WAYLON JENNINGS

1. Just the good ol' boys, _____ nev-er mean-in' no harm, _____ beats all _____ you've ev - er saw, been in trou - ble with the law since the day they was born. _____ 2. Straight -'nin' the curve, _____

Verse 2:
Straight'nin' the curve, flat'nin' the hills.
Someday the mountains might get 'em,
But the law never will. *(To Chorus:)*

Verses 3 & 4: (Instrumental solos)

Verse 5:
I'm a good ol' boy.
You know, my momma loves me,
But she don't understand.
They keep a'showin' my hands,
And not my face on T.V.
(Laughs) Hah, hah.

THE HAPPIEST GIRL IN THE WHOLE U.S.A.

Words and Music by
DONNA FARGO

The Happiest Girl in the Whole U.S.A. - 4 - 1

HARPER VALLEY P.T.A.

Words and Music by
TOM T. HALL

Moderately (with a heavy beat)

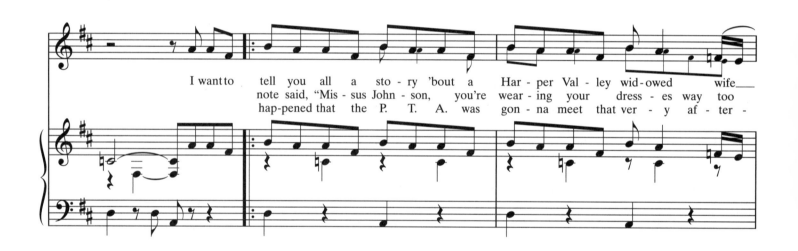

I want to tell you all a sto-ry 'bout a Har-per Val-ley wid-owed wife___
note said, "Mis-sus John-son, you're wear-ing your dress-es way too
hap-pened that the P. T. A. was gon-na meet that ver-y af-ter-

high.
noon.

who had a teen-age daugh-ter who at
It's re-port-ed you've been drink-ing and a-
They were sure sur-prised when Mis-sus John-son

Harper Valley P.T.A. - 4 - 1

tend - ed Har - per Val - ley Jun - ior High.
run - nin' 'round with men and go - ing wild.
wore her min - i - skirt in - to the room.

Well, her
And we
And as she

D7

daugh - ter came home_ one af - ter - noon, and did - n't e - ven stop to play.
don't be - lieve you ought to be a - bring - ing up your lit - tle girl this way."
walked up to the black - board, I still re - call the words she had to say;

G7   A7

She said, "Mom, I got_ a note_ here from the Har - per Val - ley P. T. A."_
It was signed by the sec - re - tar - y, Har - per Val - ley P. T. A._
she said, "I'd like to ad - dress this meet - ing of the Har - per Val - ley P. T.

1.2.   3.
D7   B♭7

A."   Well, it
The
"Well, there's

Bob - by Tay - lor, sit - tin' there, and sev - en times he's asked me for a date;
Har - per could - n't be here 'cause he stayed too long at Kel - ly's Bar a - gain,

Mis - sus Tay - lor sure seems__ to use__ a lot of ice when - ev - er he's a -
and if you smell Shir - ley Thomp - son's breath, you'll find she's had a lit - tle nip of

way."
gin."

"And Mis - ter Bak - er, can you tell us why your
"Then you have the nerve to tell me you
would - n't put you on be - cause it

sec - re - tar - y had to leave this town,
think that as a moth - er I'm not fit.
real - ly did, it hap - pened just this way,

and should - n't
Well, this is
the day my

To Coda ✛

Wid - ow Jones be told to keep her win - dow shades all pulled com - plete - ly down?"__
just a lit - tle Pey - ton Place, and you're all Har - per Val - ley hyp - o - crites."__
ma - ma socked it to the Har - per Val - ley P. T. A.

1.   2.   *D.S.* 𝄋 *al Coda*   ✛ *Coda*

"Well, Mis - ter   No, I   The day my

ma - ma socked it to the Har - per Val - ley P. T. A._____

HIGH NOON
(Do Not Forsake Me)

Lyrics by
NED WASHINGTON

Music by
DIMITRI TIOMKIN

Moderately

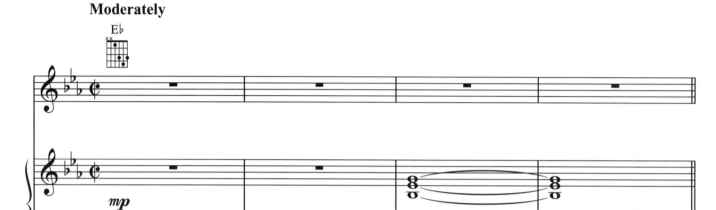

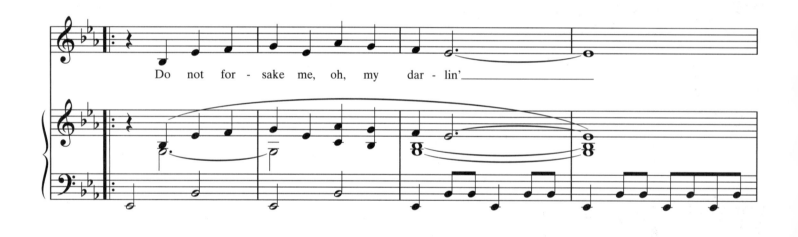

Do not for - sake me, oh, my dar - lin'

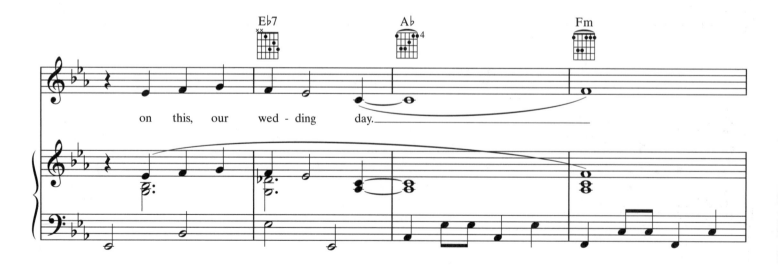

on this, our wed - ding day.

High Noon - 6 - 1

Look at that big hand move a - long___ near - in' high noon.

He made a vow while in state's pris - on, vowed it would be my life or his - 'n'

I'm not a - fraid of death but, oh,___ what will I do if you

leave me? Do not for - sake me, oh, my

I CROSS MY HEART

Words and Music by
STEVE DORFF and ERIC KAZ

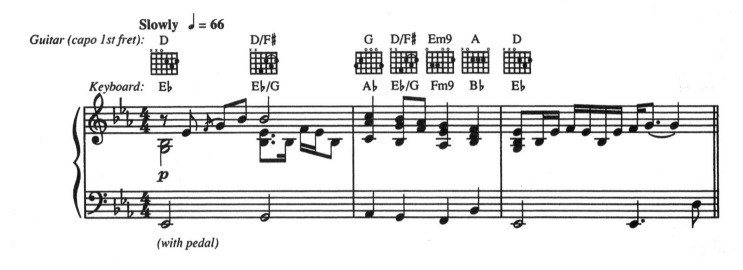

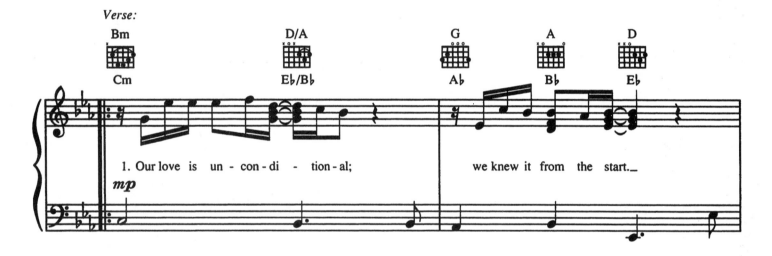

1. Our love is un-con-di-tion-al; we knew it from the start.

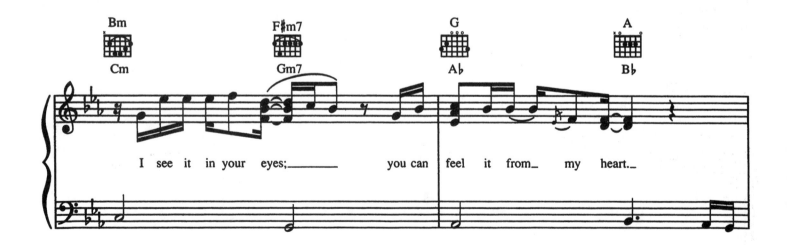

I see it in your eyes;___ you can feel it from___ my heart.___

I Cross My Heart - 4 - 1

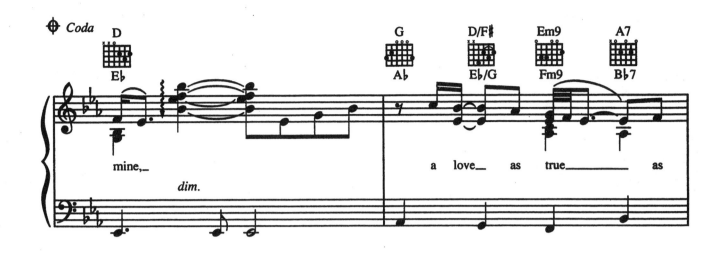

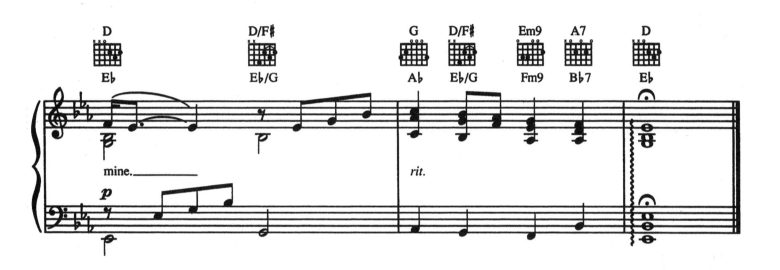

Verse 2:
You will always be the miracle
That makes my life complete;
And as long as there's a breath in me,
I'll make yours just as sweet.
As we look into the future,
It's as far as we can see,
So let's make each tomorrow
Be the best that it can be.
(To Chorus:)

I'M GONNA SIT RIGHT DOWN
AND WRITE MYSELF A LETTER

Words by
JOE YOUNG

Music by
FRED E. AHLERT

I'm Gonna Sit Right Down and Write Myself a Letter - 2 - 1

ISLANDS IN THE STREAM

Words and Music by
BARRY GIBB, MAURICE GIBB
and ROBIN GIBB

Ba - by, when I met you, there was peace un - known.___ I set out to get you with a

I can't live with - out you if the love has gone.___ Ev - 'ry - thing is noth - ing when you

fine - tooth comb. I was soft in - side;___ there___ was some - thing go - ing on.___

got no one, and you walk in the night,___ slow - ly los - ing sight of the

Islands in the Stream - 5 - 1

LET ME TELL YOU ABOUT LOVE

Words and Music by
PAUL KENNERLY, BRENT MAHER
and CARL LEE PERKINS

Bright country beat ♩ = 108

1. Well, ev-er since the day that time be-gan,__ there's
2.3. *See additional lyrics*

been this thing 'tween a wom-an and a man. Well, I don't know,__ but I

122

Instrumental solo:

D.S. 𝄋

3. Now,

✛ *Coda*

G7   F#7

Let me tell you a - bout

Verse 2:
Bonaparte and Josephine, I believe they had a pretty good scene,
Till she said, "Bonny Boy, we're through." That's when he met his Waterloo.
Julie Baby and Romeo fell in love and stole the show.
I know they are history, but there ain't been nothing like you and me.
(To Chorus:)

Verse 3:
Now, Sheba, she was a beauty queen, prettiest thing that you ever have seen.
Solomon, he was mighty wise, but Sheba, she done caught his eye.
The world would be in a dreadful fix if it wasn't for the love between cats and chicks.
This world wouldn't amount to much without a hug, a kiss, and a tender touch.
(To Chorus:)

IT'S FIVE O'CLOCK SOMEWHERE

Words and Music by
DONALD ROLLINS
and JIM BROWN

sun is hot___ and that___ ole clock___ is mov-in' slow and so
this lunch break___ is gon - na take___ all af - ter - noon and half

It's Five O'Clock Somewhere - 6 - 1

Chorus:

Chorus:

Repeat ad lib. and fade

(Dialogue - See additional lyrics)

Dialogue:
Jimmy: What time zone am I on? What country am I in?
Alan: It doesn't matter. It's five o'clock somewhere.
Jimmy: It's always on five in Margaritaville, come to think of it.
Alan: I heard that.
Jimmy: You've been there, haven't you?
Alan: Yes, sir.
Jimmy: I've seen your boat there.
Alan: I've been to Margaritaville a few times.
Jimmy: All right. That's good.
Alan: Stumbled my way back.
Jimmy: OK. Just want to make sure you can keep it between the navigational beacons.
Alan: Between the bouys. I got it.
Jimmy: All right. It's five o'clock. Let's go somewhere.
Alan: I'm ready. Crank it up.
Jimmy: Let's get out of here.
Alan: I'm gone.

IT'S JUST A MATTER OF TIME

Words and Music by
CLYDE OTIS, BROOK BENTON
and BELFORD HENDRICKS

Moderately slow ♩. = 66

Bridge:

I _____ know you'll pass my ___ way a-gain.

It's just a mat-ter ___ of time. ___ Af-ter I

gave you ___ ev-'ry-thing ___ I had, ___

you laughed and called ___ me a clown. ___ Re-mem-ber

JAMBALAYA
(ON THE BAYOU)

Words and Music by
HANK WILLIAMS

Jambalaya - 2 - 1

CHORUS

JAM-BA-LA-YA and a craw-fish pie and fil-let gum-bo ___

'Cause to-night I'm gon-na see my ma cher a-mi-o ___ Pick gui-

tar, fill fruit jar and be gay-o ___ Son of a gun, we'll have big

1.2. fun on the bay-ou ___ **2.** Thi-bo- bay-ou ___ **3.**

Verse 3:
Settle down far from town, get me a pirogue
And I'll catch all the fish in the bayou
Swap my mon to buy Yvonne what she need-o
Son of a gun, we'll have big fun on the bayou

LET ME BE THERE

Words and Music by
JOHN ROSTILL

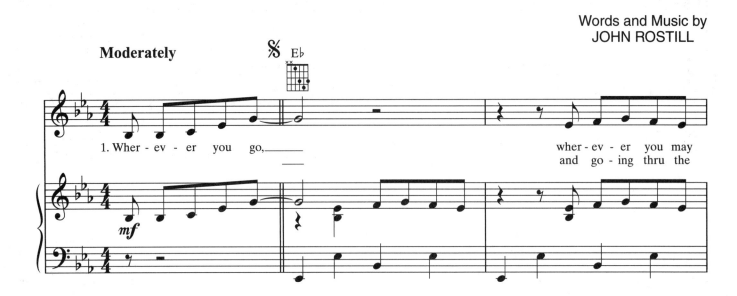

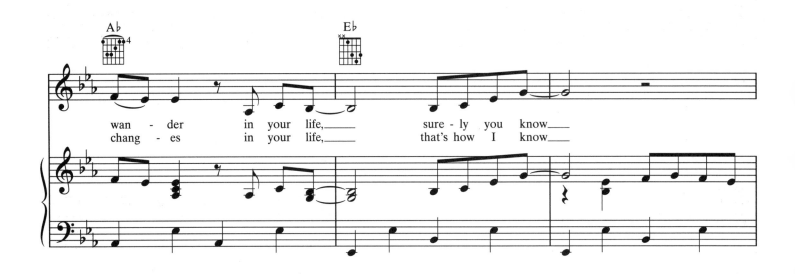

Let Me Be There - 4 - 1

LOST IN THE FIFTIES TONIGHT
(IN THE STILL OF THE NIGHT)

Words and Music by TROY SEALS,
FRED PARRIS and MIKE REID

Close your eyes___ ba - by, fol - low my heart;___ call on the mem - 'ries___
These prec - ious___ hours___ we know can't sur - vive,___ but love's all that mat - ters___

here in the dark.___ We'll let the mag - ic___ take___ us a - way,___
while the past is a - live.___ Now and for al - ways,___ time___ dis - ap - pears,___

Lost in the Fifties Tonight - 3 - 1

THE MOST BEAUTIFUL GIRL

Words and Music by
NORRIS WILSON, BILLY SHERRILL
and RORY BOURKE

Moderately ♩ = 108

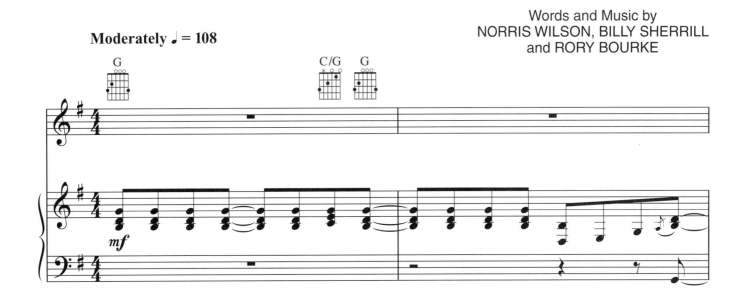

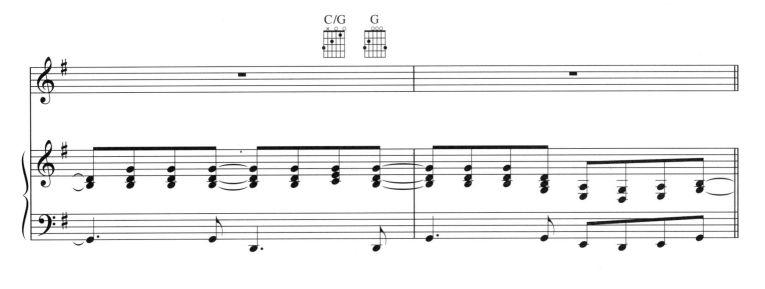

Chorus:

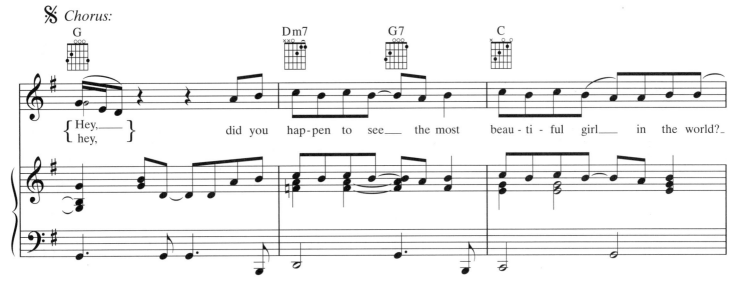

{ Hey, } did you hap-pen to see__ the most beau-ti-ful girl__ in the world?__
{ hey, }

The Most Beautiful Girl - 5 - 1

To Coda

my____ ba - by. Oh,_____ won't you tell

her____ that I love____ her?__

Verse:

I woke up this morn - in',____ re - al - ized____ what I had

done. I stood a-lone in the cold grey dawn;__ I

LOVE IN THE FIRST DEGREE

Words and Music by
JIM HURT and TIM DUBOIS

Love in the First Degree - 4 - 1

Love in the First Degree - 4 - 4

LOVE WITHOUT END, AMEN

Words and Music by
AARON G. BARKER

Moderately, with a beat

just like I'd re - hearsed, _____ and then I
test - ed to the end, _____

stood there on those trem - blin' knees___ and wait - ed for ___ the worst.___
took my Dad-dy's se - cret and I passed it on ___ to him.___

_____ And he said,} "Let me tell ___ you a se - cret ___ a -
_____ I said,}

bout a fa - ther's ___ love, a se - cret that ___ my _____ Dad-dy said ___ was

never let____ me in._____ And then

some-where from the oth-er side I heard these words a-gain.____

_____ And they said, Let me tell____ you a se-cret____ a-

bout____ a fa-ther's____ love, a se-cret that____ my____ dad-dy said____ was

LOVE'S BEEN A LITTLE BIT HARD ON ME

Words and Music by
GARY BURR

Moderately Bright ♩= 138

A   D/A   E/A   A   D   E   A

Verse: A   D   E   A   D

1. I've got noth-ing to be 'shamed of; love's been a lit-tle bit
2.3. (see additional lyrics)

E   A   D   E   A

hard on me. If I shy a-way it's on-ly be-cause; love's

Love's Been a Little Bit Hard on Me - 4 - 1

Love's Been a Little Bit Hard on Me - 4 - 2

162

Love's Been a Little Bit Hard on Me - 4 - 3

Coda

hard _____ on me.

Repeat ad lib and fade

Verse II:
I can remember when it's been so much;
Love's been a little bit hard on me.
I shy away at the slightest touch;
Love's been a little bit hard on me.

Verse III:
I'll be back when I calm my fears;
Love's been a little bit hard on me.
See you around in a thousand years;
Love's been a little bit hard on me.

LUCILLE

Words and Music by
ROGER BOWLING and
HAL BYNUM

In a moderate country 3

Verses 1 & 2:

1. In a bar in To - le - do a-
(2.) mir - ror I saw him and

cross from the de - pot,___ on a bar - stool she took off her ring.___
I close - ly watched him,___ I thought how he looked out of place.___

I thought I'd get clos - er, so I walked on___ o - ver, I
He came to the wom - an who sat there be - side me, he

Lucille - 6 - 1

Chorus:

2. In the turned to the wom-an and said: "You picked a fine time to leave___ me, Lu-cille, with four hun-gry chil-dren and a crop in the field. I've had some bad times,___ lived through some sad times,___ but this time your hurt-in' won't

MARGARITAVILLE

Words and Music by
JIMMY BUFFETT

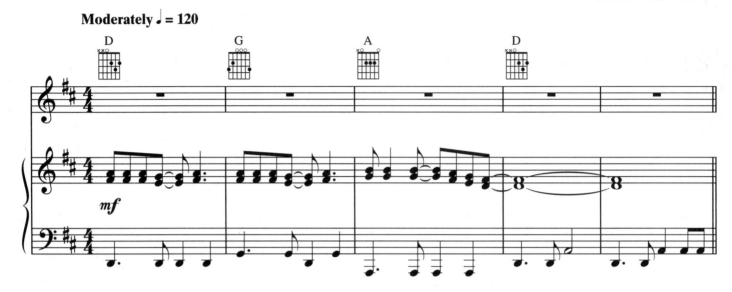

Verse:

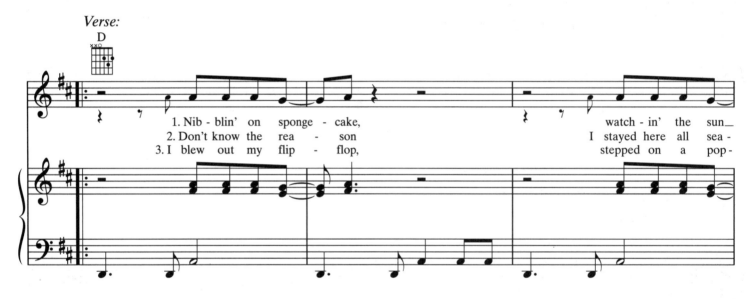

1. Nib - blin' on sponge - cake, watch - in' the sun__
2. Don't know the rea - son I stayed here all sea -
3. I blew out my flip - flop, stepped on a pop -

__ bake; all of those tour - ists cov - ered with oil.__
son with noth - ing to show__ but this brand - new tat - too.__
top; cut my heel,__ had to cruise on back home.__

Margaritaville - 4 - 1

MR. BOJANGLES

Words and Music by
JERRY JEFF WALKER

Moderately slow waltz, in one ♩. = 50

Verse 1:

knew a man, Bo - jan - gles, and he'd dance____ for you

in worn out____ shoes,

sil - ver hair and rag - ged shirt and bag - gy pants, the

old soft___ shoe. He jumped so high,___

___ he jumped so high,___ and then he'd

light - ly touch___ down.___ 2. I

𝄋 *Verses 2–5:*

met him in a cell___ in New Or - leans;___ I was

3.4.5. See additional lyrics

down and out.___

He looked to me to be___ the eyes___

___ of age,

as the smoke ran___ out.

He talked of life,___

he talked of life;___

D.S. %

jan - gles,

dance.

dance.

rit. poco a poco

molto rit.

freely

Verse 3:
He said his name, Bojangles, and he danced a lick
Across the cell.
He grabbed his pants and feathered stance, whoa, he jumped so high,
And then he clicked his heels.
He let go a laugh, he let go a laugh,
Shook back his clothes all around.
(To Chorus:)

Verse 4:
He danced for those at minstrel shows and county fairs
Throughout the South.
He spoke through tears of fifteen years, how his dog and him
Traveled about.
The dog up and died, he up and died.
After twenty years, he still grieved.

Verse 5:
He said, "I dance now at ev'ry chance in honky-tonks
For drinks and tips.
But most the time I spend behind these county bars,
Because I drinks a bit."
He shook his head, and as he shook his head,
I heard someone ask him, "Please, please."
(To Chorus:)

PASSIONATE KISSES

Words and Music by
LUCINDA WILLIAMS

Moderately fast

Is — it too — much too ask, — I want a com-fort-able bed — that won't

(See additional lyrics)

hurt my back? — Food — to fill me up, — and

Passionate Kisses - 5 - 1

Additional Lyrics

2. Is it too much to demand,
   I want a full house and a rock 'n' roll band?
   Pens that won't run out of ink,
   And cool quiet time to think.
   (To Chorus)

3. Do I want too much,
   Am I going overboard to want that touch?
   I shout it out to the night,
   Give me what I deserve 'cause it's my right.
   (To Chorus)

MY SPECIAL ANGEL

Words and Music by
JIMMY DUNCAN

My Special Angel - 2 - 1

NEAR YOU

Words by
KERMIT GOELL

Music by
FRANCIS CRAIG

PANCHO AND LEFTY

Words and Music by
TOWNES VAN ZANDT

1. Liv - ing on the road, _____ my friend, _____
2. 3. 4. *(See additional lyrics)*

Pancho and Lefty - 4 - 2

D.S.(3rd Verse)
D.SS.(Instr.)
D.S.(4th Verse)
D.SS. al Coda

To Coda

out of kind-ness I __ sup-pose.

Coda

pose.

rit.

Verse 2:
Pancho was a bandit boy,
His horse was fast as polished steel.
He wore his gun outside his pants,
For all the honest world to feel.
Well, Pancho met his match, you know,
On the deserts down in Mexico.
Nobody heard his dying word,
Ah, but that's the way it goes.

Verse 3:
Lefty, he can't sing the blues,
All night long like he used to.
The dust that Pancho bit down south,
Ended up in Lefty's mouth.
The day they laid poor Pancho low,
Lefty split for Ohio.
Where he got the bread to go,
There ain't nobody know.

Verse 4:
The poets tell how Pancho felt,
And Lefty's living in a cheap hotel;
The desert's quiet, and Cleveland's cold,
And so the story ends we're told.
Pancho needs your prayers, it's true,
And save a few for Lefty, too.
He only did what he had to do,
And now, he's growing old.

PAPER ROSES

Words and Music by
FRITZ SPIELMAN and JANICE TORRE

Paper Roses - 2 - 1

send the kind that you re-mind me of.
send the kind that you re-mind me of.
just a stiff and ar-ti-fi-cial pose.
is-n't an-y sweet-ness in your heart.

CHORUS

Pa-per Ro-ses,____ Pa-per Ro-ses,____ Oh how real those ros-es

seem to be!_____ But they're on-ly____ im-i-ta-tion____

Like your im-i-ta-tion love for me.____ (Boy)2. Your
(Girl)3. I

me._____ Like your im-i-ta-tion love for me.____

Paper Roses - 2 - 2

PLEASE HELP ME, I'M FALLING

(In Love With You)

Words and Music by
HAL BLAIR and DON ROBERTSON

Moderate country two-beat

Please help me, I'm fall - ing_____
oth - er_____
fall - ing_____

____ in love with____ you.
____ whose arms have grown cold._____
____ and that would be sin._____

Close the door to temp -
But I prom - ised for -
Close the door to temp -

Please Help Me, I'm Falling - 2 - 2

RHINESTONE COWBOY

Words and Music by
LARRY WEISS

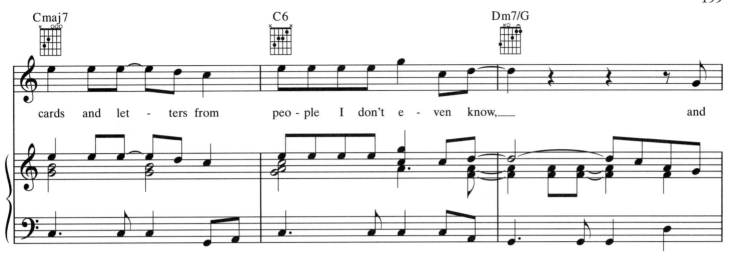

cards and let - ters from peo - ple I don't e - ven know,___ and

of - fers com-ing o - ver the phone.

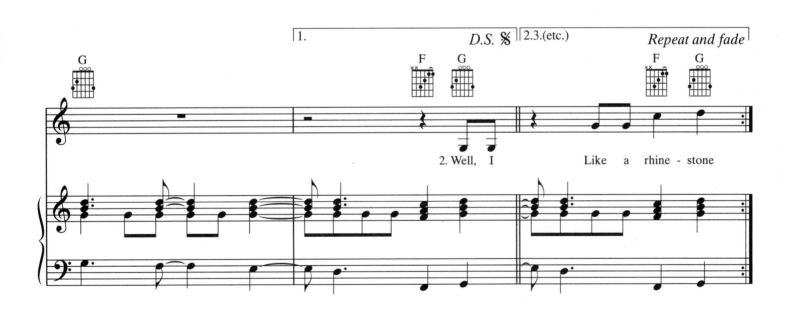

D.S. 𝄋   Repeat and fade

2. Well, I   Like a rhine - stone

SEVEN SPANISH ANGELS

Words and Music by
EDDIE SETSER and TROY SEALS

He looked down in-to___ her brown eyes and said, "Say a prayer_ for me." She
down and picked_ the gun up that lay smok-in' in____ his hand._ She said,

threw her arms_ a-round him, whis-pered, "God will keep_ us free."___ They could
"Fa-ther, please_ for-give me, I can't make it with-out my man."___ And she

SHE GOT THE GOLD MINE
(And I Got the Shaft)

Words and Music by
TIM DUBOIS

(Spoken) 1. Well, I guess

Verse:

it was back in Sixty-three, when eatin' my cookin' got the better of me, so I asked

2.3.4.5. See additional lyrics

this little girl I was goin' with to be my wife. Well, she said she

4. She got__ the gold - shaft._____

Repeat ad lib. and fade

C   F

(Spoken ad lib.)

f

Verse 2:
Well, the first few years weren't all that bad.
I'll never forget the good times we had,
'Cause I'm reminded every month
When I send her the child support.
Well, it wasn't too long till the lust all died.
And I'll admit I wasn't too surprised
The day I came home and found my suitcase
Sittin' out on the porch.

Verse 3:
Well, I tried to get in, but she changed the locks.
Then I found this note taped on the mailbox that said,
"Good-bye, Turkey! My attorney will be in touch."
So I decided right then and there,
I was gonna do what's right and give her her fair share.
But, brother, I didn't know her share was gonna be that much!
(To Chorus:)

Verse 4:
Now, listen; you ain't heard nothin' yet.
Why, they gave her the color television set,
And they gave her the house, the kids, and both of the cars.
Then they start talkin' about child support,
Alimony, and the cost of the court;
Didn't take me long to figure out how far in the toilet I was!

Verse 5:
I'm tellin' ya, they have made a mistake,
'Cause it adds up to more than this cowboy makes.
Besides, everything I ever had worth takin',
They've already took.
While she's livin' like a queen on alimony,
I'm workin' two shifts and eatin' bologna;
Askin' myself, "Why didn't you just learn how to cook?"
(To Chorus:)

SIOUX CITY SUE

Words by
RAY FREEDMAN

Music by
DICK THOMAS

Moderate country two-beat

Verse:

1. I drove a herd of cat-tle down from
(2.) asked her if she had a beau; she
(3.) I'm ad-mit-ting, I-o-way, I

old Ne-bras-ka way. That's how I come to
said, "Yes, quite a few." But still I come start-ed
owe a lot to you, 'cause I come from Ne-

be in the state of I-o-way. I
court-in' my sweet Sioux Cit-y Sue. The
bras-ka to find Sioux Cit-y Sue. I'm

Chorus:

STAND BY YOUR MAN

Words and Music by
TAMMY WYNETTE and BILLY SHERRILL

Stand By Your Man - 5 - 1

SIXTEEN TONS

Words and Music by
MERLE TRAVIS

Sixteen Tons - 2 - 1

THE SWEETEST THING
(I'VE EVER KNOWN)

Words and Music by
OTHA YOUNG

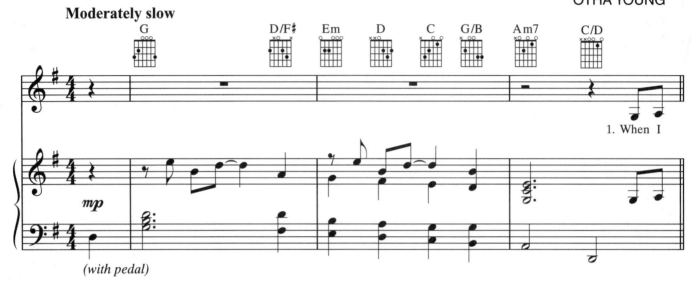

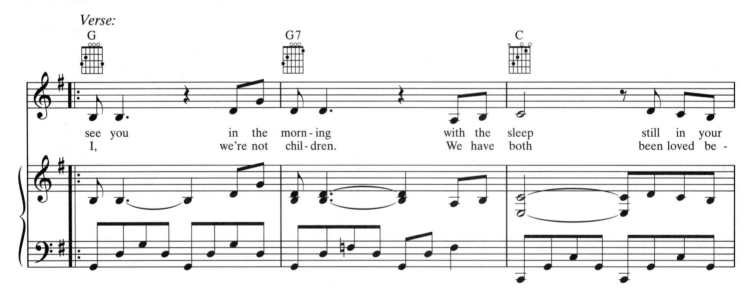

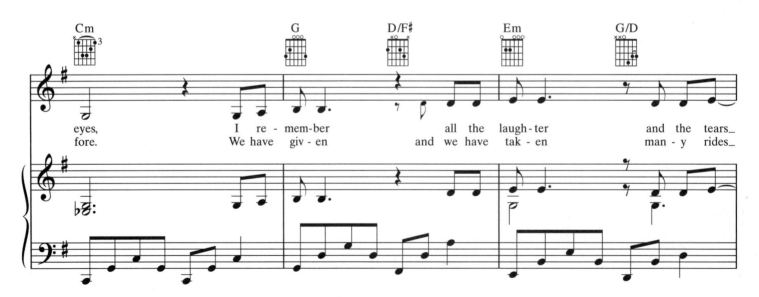

The Sweetest Thing - 4 - 1

TAKE THIS JOB AND SHOVE IT

Words and Music by
DAVID ALLEN COE

Take This Job And Shove It - 3 - 3

THANK GOD I'M A COUNTRY BOY

Words and Music by
JOHN MARTIN SOMMERS

Moderately

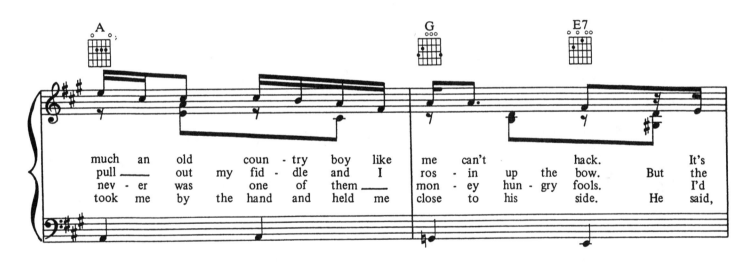

Thank God I'm a Country Boy - 3 - 1

TWO OF A KIND, WORKIN' ON A FULL HOUSE

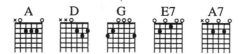

Words and Music by
BOBBY BOYD, WARREN DALE HAYNES
and DENNIS ROBBINS

Two of a Kind, Workin' on a Full House - 3 - 1

Yeah, we're two of a kind,___ work-in' on___ a full

house. 2. She wakes___ house. 1. Yeah, a pick-

Bridge:

-up truck___ is her lim-ou-sine.___ And her fa-vor-ite dress is her

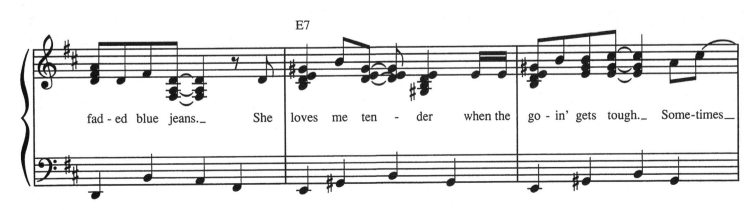

fad-ed blue jeans.___ She loves me ten-der when the go-in' gets tough.___ Some-times___

Verse 2:
She wakes me every mornin'
With a smile and a kiss.
Her strong country lovin' is hard to resist.
She's my easy lovin' woman,
I'm her hard-workin' man, no doubt.
Yeah, we're two of a kind
Workin' on a full house. *(To Bridge:)*

Verse 3:
Lord, I need that little woman
Like the crops need rain.
She's my honeycomb, and I'm her sugar cane.
We really fit together
If you know what I'm talkin' about.
Yeah, we're two of a kind
Workin' on a full house. *(To Bridge 2:)*

Bridge 2:
This time I found a keeper, I made up my mind.
Lord, the perfect combination is her heart and mine.
The sky's the limit, no hill is too steep.
We're playin' for fun, but we're playin' for keeps.

Verse 4:
So draw the curtain, honey.
Turn the lights down low.
We'll find some country music on the radio.
I'm yours and you're mine.
Hey, that's what it's all about.
Yeah, we're two of a kind
Workin' on a full house.
Lordy mama, we'll be two of a kind
Workin' on a full house.

WALK RIGHT BACK

Words and Music by
SONNY CURTIS

Moderately bright Country beat

want you to tell me why you walked out on

me. I'm so lone-some ev-'ry day.

Walk Right Back - 3 - 1

WALKING THE FLOOR OVER YOU

Words and Music by
ERNEST TUBB

Chorus:

A WHITE SPORT COAT
(And a Pink Carnation)

Words and Music by
MARTY ROBBINS

Moderate country swing ♩ = 69

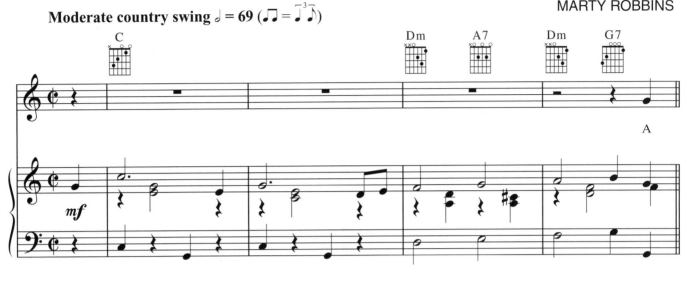

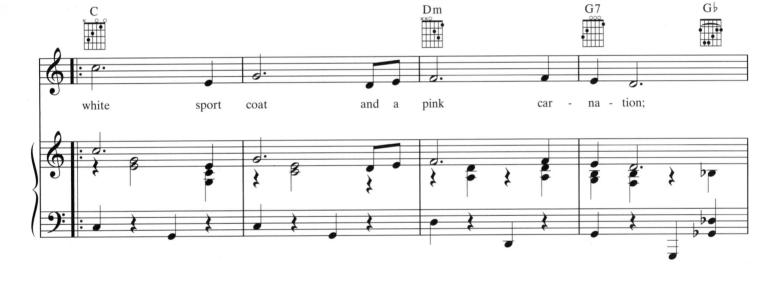

white   sport   coat   and a   pink   car - na - tion;

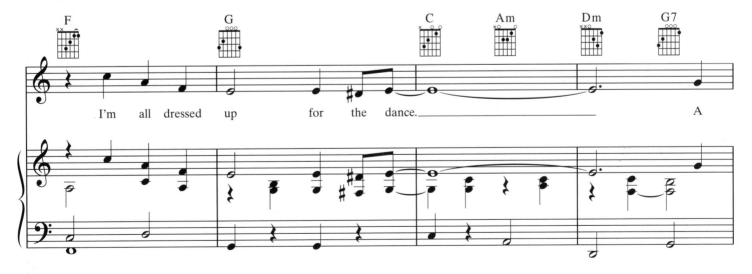

I'm all dressed up   for the dance._____

WASTED DAYS AND WASTED NIGHTS

Words and Music by
HUEY P. MEAUX

Wasted Days and Wasted Nights - 2 - 2

WHAT'S MADE MILWAUKEE FAMOUS
(Has Made a Loser Out of Me)

Words and Music by
GLENN SUTTON

Moderate country shuffle ♩ = 100

It's late and she's wait-ing, and I know I should go home. But ev-'ry time I start to leave

What's Made Milwaukee Famous - 4 - 1

WHOLE LOTTA SHAKIN' GOING ON

Words and Music by
DAVID WILLIAMS

Moderately fast rock and roll ♩ = 160

1. Come_

𝄋 *Verse:*

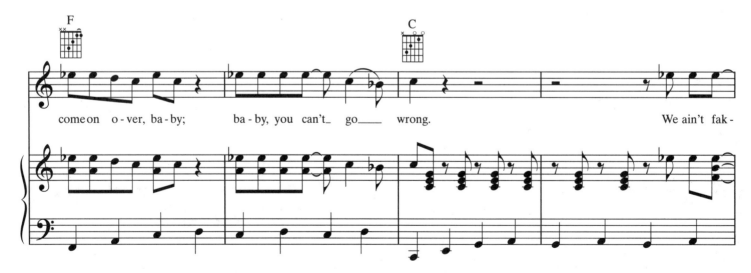

_ on o - ver, ba - by, whole_ lot - ta shak-in' go-in' on. Yes, I said

2.4. *See additional lyrics*
3. *Guitar solo ad lib.*

come on o - ver, ba - by; ba - by, you can't_ go_ wrong. We ain't fak-

Whole Lotta Shakin' Going On - 5 - 1

Piano solo:

*Now, let's get down
real low one time now.*

Shake, ba - by, shake.___

ba - by, shake.___ Come on o - ver, whole___ lot - ta shak-

in'___ go - in' on._____

Verse 2:
Well, I said come along, my baby, we got chicken in the corn.
Woo-huh, come along, my baby, really got the bull by the horn.
We ain't fakin', whole lotta shakin' goin' on.
(To Chorus:)

Verse 4:
Well, I said come along, my baby, we got chicken in the barn,
whose barn, what barn, my barn.
Come along, my baby, really got the bull by the horn.
We ain't fakin', whole lotta shakin' goin' on.

Chorus 2:
(Spoken:)
Easy now. Shake.
Ah, shake it, baby.
Yeah, you can shake it one time for me.
(Sung:)
Yeah-huh-huh-ha-ha, come along, my baby,
Whole lotta shakin' goin' on.
(To Chorus 3:)

YOU DON'T KNOW ME

Words and Music by
CINDY WALKER
and EDDY ARNOLD

You Don't Know Me - 3 - 1

WINGS OF A DOVE

Words and Music by
BOB FERGUSON

Wings of a Dove - 2 - 1

THE YELLOW ROSE OF TEXAS

Traditional

YOU LIGHT UP MY LIFE

Words and Music by
JOE BROOKS

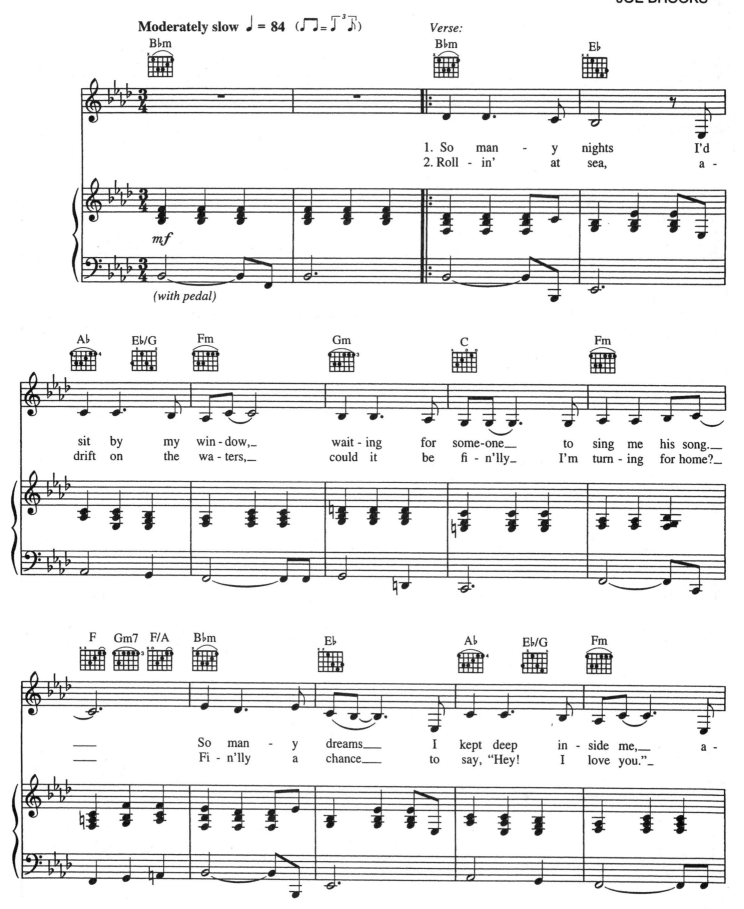

You Light Up My Life - 3 - 1

YOU NEEDED ME

Words and Music by
RANDY GOODRUM

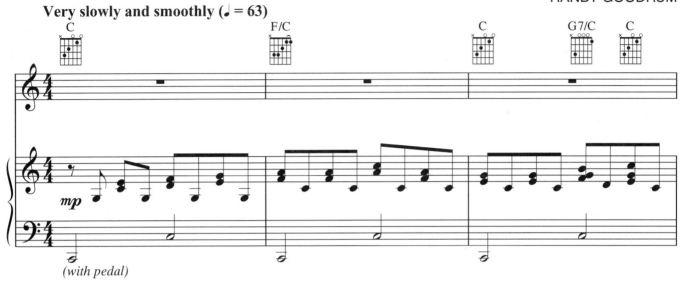

I cried a tear, you wiped it dry. I was con-

fused, you cleared my mind. I sold my soul, you bought it

back for me,___ and held it up and gave it dig-ni-ty.___ Some-how you

need-ed me. You gave me strength to stand a-lone a-gain,_ to face the

world out on my own a-gain._ You put me high up-on a

ped-es-tal,___ so high that I___ can al-most see___ e-ter-ni-ty.___ You

YOU LOOK SO GOOD IN LOVE

Words and Music by
RORY BOURKE, KERRY CHATER
and GLEN BALLARD

You Look So Good in Love - 4 - 1

YOUR CHEATIN' HEART

Words and Music by
HANK WILLIAMS

Your Cheatin' Heart - 3 - 1